The Autist's Guide to Narcissistic Abuse

The Autist's Guide to Narcissistic Abuse

Volume One:
The Enablers

Arthur Quintalino

Autist Publications
Lancaster, 2025

The Autist's Guide to Narcissistic Abuse
Volume One: The Enablers
© 2025 Arthur Quintalino, some rights reserved.

Supplemental Permission for Clinician Use

In addition to the CC BY-NC 4.0 license, the author grants licensed mental-health clinicians (e.g., psychologists, psychiatrists, clinical social workers, domestic violence or other professional counselors, marriage & family therapists) a no-fee permission to:

1. Reproduce and distribute this work (and reasonable adaptations or translations) to active clients in the ordinary course of paid clinical practice, including individual therapy, group therapy, workshops, and psychoeducational groups;
2. Incorporate excerpts in session materials, homework handouts, and slide decks used with clients;
3. Make reasonable adaptations (e.g., adding practice-specific contact info, tailoring examples, translating) provided (a) attribution to the author is retained, and (b) adaptations are clearly labeled as such.

This permission does not authorize:

1. Selling the work (or adaptations) as a standalone product;
   (e.g., a book, course, or paid download);
2. Posting the full work or adapted versions for unrestricted public download;
3. Sublicensing or granting broader commercial rights to others.

All uses must include the attribution above.

For permissions beyond this scope (publishers, courses, large-scale distribution), contact: licensing@TheAutistsGuide.com

Disclaimer

This handbook is for educational support. It is not legal, medical, or therapeutic advice.
No warranty is expressed or implied.

Media Contact: books@TheAutistsGuide.com

First Printing, December 2025

ISBN-13 979-8-9932881-3-0

To my children:
Who, through shadow and ice,
helped me find what I had lost

To Leo:
For rescuing me
as much as I rescued him.

Table of Contents

AUTHOR'S NOTES IX

    ON LANGUAGE AND TERMINOLOGY IX
    ON FLUID VISCOSITY IX
    ON NOUNS, ADJECTIVES, AND DIAGNOSES IX
    ON SOURCES X
    ON GOING IT ALONE X
    ON THE POEMS XI
    ON PAYMENT AND DISTRIBUTION XI

UNBROKEN XIII

INTRODUCTION 1

I. ARCHITECTURES OF COMPLICITY 3

    THE HOT SEAT: A LESSON IN GENERATIONAL CRUELTY 5
    A TAXONOMY 5
    THE PASSIVE ENABLER: MASTERS OF STRATEGIC BLINDNESS 5
    THE ACTIVE ENABLER: EXTENDED ARMS OF ABUSE 6
    COVERT ENABLERS: FALSE ALLIES IN SHEEP'S CLOTHING 7
    INSTITUTIONAL ENABLERS: SANCTIONED COMPLICITY 8
    MALIGNANT ENABLERS: ARCHITECTS OF SECONDARY ABUSE 9
    TAKING A MOMENT: MAP THE PATTERNS IN YOUR LIFE 11

II. THE PSYCHOLOGY OF COLLUSION 13

    SEARCHING FOR ANSWERS 15
    FEAR-BASED ENABLERS: YOUR SACRIFICE, THEIR SAFETY 15
    FAVOR-SEEKING ENABLERS: COMPETING FOR CRUMBS 16
    TRAUMA-BONDED ENABLERS: THE CAPTIVE COLLABORATORS 17
    ARCHITECT ENABLERS: BUILD ON YOUR WOUNDS 18

III. THE TRAUMA OF BETRAYAL 21

    THE FIRST CUT'S NOT ALWAYS THE DEEPEST 23
    THE NEUROLOGICAL SIGNATURE OF SYSTEMATIC BETRAYAL 23
    THE TEMPORAL COLLAPSE OF BETRAYAL DISCOVERY 24
    THE METABOLIC COST OF BETRAYAL RECOGNITION 25
    THE EPISTEMOLOGICAL VIOLENCE OF GASLIT REALITY 26
    THE IMMUNOLOGICAL METAPHOR 27
    HEALING THE BETRAYAL WOUND 27

DANCING LESSONS 31

IV. THE PLAYBOOK 33

THE NORMALIZATION CAMPAIGN..35
BLAME SHIFTING AND VICTIM TARGETING...................................35
INFORMATION WARFARE..36
RECOVERY SABOTAGE 37
THE ENABLER RECOGNITION CHECKLIST 38
SAMPLE SCRIPTS FOR BOUNDARY SETTING 40
WARNING SIGNS SOMEONE IS BECOMING AN ENABLER............41
GREEN FLAGS: IDENTIFYING GENUINE SUPPORT 42
THE ULTIMATE GREEN FLAG:...43
TAKING A MOMENT: PRACTICE MAKES ... DOABLE 43

V. THE MIRROR CHECK 45
RECOGNIZING YOURSELF IN THE SYSTEM................................47
THE GOSSIP GATEWAY 47
THE TRIANGULATION TEST 48
SCRIPTS FOR DECLINING PARTICIPATION 49
THE REHABILITATION PROTOCOL 50
THE DEEPER RECOGNITION 50
TAKING A MOMENT: CHECK YOURSELF 51

VI. STRATEGIC RESPONSE 53
PROTECTING YOURSELF FROM THE NETWORK 55
OPERATIONAL SECURITY: MAPPING THE NETWORK 57

VII. THE PATH FORWARD... 61
EMBRACING NECESSARY LOSSES 63
THE RECKONING 63

AFTER 67

GLOSSARY... 68

BIBLIOGRAPHY 73

APPENDIX.. 77
FOR CLINICIANS & HELPERS: A QUICK REFERENCE 77

ACKNOWLEDGEMENTS... 79

Author's Notes

On Language and Terminology

When it comes to dealing with—and healing from—narcissists and those who give them aid, what I've found is that some of the ideas (and hence, their names) originate not from renowned clinicians—though many do—but from the ever-growing community dedicated to healing from narcissistic abuse and helping others do the same. As such, many terms, acronyms, and methods you'll see everywhere from social media to professional settings have interesting-sounding names, like "flying monkey," DARVO (Freyd), JADE (Al-Anon), FOG (Forward), or stones of varying color. Where used, I'll do my best to offer a brief explanation in context, but there is a glossary at the end.

On Fluid Viscosity

"Blood is thicker than water," has been a war cry of abusers and enablers alike. On this side of an arduous healing journey, I much prefer the more modern recasting of this phrase as used by Trumbull, Pustelniak, and Lindemann: "The blood of the covenant is thicker than the water of the womb," particularly because it fits with the chosen families we find ourselves with when our family of origin turns out not to be somewhere we can find safety.

On Nouns, Adjectives, and Diagnoses

In this series of books, I use the terms narcissist and abuser interchangeably to refer to perpetrators of narcissistic abuse. **Narcissist** and **narcissism** are *nouns*. **Narcissistic** is an *adjective*. **Narcissistic Personality Disorder** (NPD) is a *clinical diagnosis* with specific criteria. Like many things, narcissistic traits fall on a spectrum. Someone may exhibit several narcissistic or other Cluster B traits and still not meet criteria for NPD.

I do not diagnose individuals in these pages—I am not qualified to do so. Nothing herein is intended to be used for diagnostic purposes.

On Sources

This work draws on survivor accounts and ethnography, practitioner literature, and peer-reviewed research. Where a point appears in more than one stream, I have tried to cross-reference representative voices (e.g., survivor-practitioner observations alongside object-relations and betrayal-trauma theory).

On Going it Alone

If you are unfortunate enough to relate to things you are about to read, and you have not already sought professional assistance, *please* do that as soon as possible, provided you are in any kind of a position to do so. Don't look for a practitioner who only claims to be "trauma-informed," but one who *specializes* in narcissistic abuse, complex PTSD, and/or domestic violence. The road to healing from the types of traumas that likely led you here is one that is both long and scarred. Having a professional who understands what you're going through to guide you on that path can make all the difference.

On the Poems

Throughout this book, you'll encounter three poems—*Unbroken, Dancing Lessons,* and *After*. These aren't decorative interludes but deliberate breathing spaces, moments where the systematic analysis pauses to acknowledge what data alone cannot capture. Trauma lives in the body as much as the mind, in metaphor as much as mechanism. These poems offer a different register for processing—where pattern recognition meets emotional resonance, where the analytical mind can rest while something deeper integrates. Consider them waypoints on a difficult journey, not departures from it but essential parts of the whole.

On Payment and Distribution

As the copyright page says, this Creative Commons-licensed work may be distributed freely with attribution. It is *also* available for purchase. If this manual has been useful to you, personally or professionally, please consider supporting my ability to create future resources by purchasing a copy or subscribing to my Substack.

To that end, I pledge to donate 10% of the net proceeds from all sales of this work to organizations aiding victims of domestic violence.

More information is available at AnAutistsGuide.com

Arthur Quintalino
Lancaster, Pennsylvania
December, 2025

Unbroken

I am a survivor of the unseen —
Not of scarring wounds, but of twisted tales.
Told my mind was sharp, but my thoughts unclean,
Too wise was I? Or too crazy? Or frail?

I lived in doubt — self-taught to second-guess,
Been gaslit, shamed, and stripped of where I stood.
The ground would shift beneath each false address —
Your deals — deception. As with my childhood.

But I remain, to name what they erase.
The robed need not confirm what I still see.
I bring my history into that place —
Stronger, I raise my voice with clarity.

I do not walk in silence or alone.
My truth is mine. It stands. Let it be known.

Introduction

Everyone studies the narcissist, but it's the enablers who make their world go 'round. Behind every sustained campaign of psychological abuse stands a network of collaborators colluding with the abusive party to transform the impossible into the inevitable. If narcissists are the architects of alternate realities, they are the engineers who help reconstruct abuse as affection, cruelty as care, and boundaries as betrayal.

I learned this through *systematic* betrayal—not from the narcissists whose patterns I'd eventually mapped and understood, but from those I'd trusted to remain neutral ground—or worse, relied on for support. When someone handed over the keys to my carefully constructed sanctuary, they didn't just share a phone number. They revealed how enablers function as essential infrastructure in abuse systems, how their participation transforms individual pathology into collective persecution.

My father—thirty-plus years after escaping my mother's orbit—still couldn't resist playing messenger boy when she asked for my number. The first phone number in my life she didn't have. The first veil she'd been unable to pierce. "I didn't think it was a big deal," he said. "I only gave it to Jeff." As if there were degrees of separation between my mother and her codependently enmeshed husband. As if more than three decades of post-separation abuse hadn't taught him that there's no such thing as "only" anything when it comes to narcissistic intelligence gathering.

The systematic inversion narcissists perform—where your self-protection becomes their victimization—requires more than one person's delusion. It requires a chorus of validators, a network of nodes transmitting and amplifying the distortion until it becomes environmental. Understanding enablers isn't peripheral to recognizing abuse; *it's central to both survival and recovery.* Because while the narcissist is getting ready to push you, it's often the enabler bending down behind your knees.

I.
Architectures of Complicity

The Hot Seat: A Lesson in Generational Cruelty

The hot seat was a post-dinner torture game perfected by my maternal family. Picture an entire family gathered around while one person, chosen seemingly at random but really through a precise calculus, becomes the target of "jokes" that aren't meant for humor so much as orchestrated demolition. Questions designed to humiliate. Comparisons crafted to diminish. Laughter that *sounds* like solidarity but cuts like cold steel.

The rules were unspoken but absolute—subjects couldn't leave, nor could they defend themselves without being labeled "too sensitive," and drawing further derision. Nor could one refuse participation without becoming a target. It was systematic destruction mislabeled as family bonding, where the price of belonging was either accepting your own public evisceration while everyone watched, participated, and called it love—or joining in on the "fun," when someone else was being targeted, to keep everyone comfortable with their cruelty.

Active enablers (in this instance, the enablers belonged to my maternal grandfather) were the ones throwing the first stones, testing for weak spots, finding where to aim. They weren't drafted into service. They *volunteered*—so eager were they to prove loyalty through verbal laceration.

A Taxonomy

Seeing patterns is a dead useful skill to have. Giving names and descriptions to what's identified in those patterns grants us a shared language we, as survivors of narcissistic abuse, can use to help ourselves, and potentially our therapists, understand what it is we're dealing with.

The Passive Enabler: Masters of Strategic Blindness

The passive enabler perfects the art of selective perception. They develop a peculiar form of blindness that operates only in the presence of abuse, a convenient myopia that allows them to inhabit the same space as violence while claiming complete ignorance.

"I never saw anything troubling," one aunt would claim, despite having witnessed my mother's screaming campaigns that could be heard half a block away. This wasn't simple denial. It was architectural. By refusing to see, she created plausible deniability that protected her position in the family system—abandoning the rest of us to drown in its dysfunction.

You want to know what strategic blindness looks like today? Picture holiday dinners where a child gets eviscerated for breathing wrong while aunts and uncles suddenly develop fascinating relationships with their phones. Picture "I was in the bathroom" becoming a multi-decade alibi. Picture selective deafness so profound it could qualify for disability benefits, and blindness rivaled only by seasoned diner waitstaff. Naturally, they are only afflicted when a victim is under attack.

Their phrases become predictable: "I stay out of it." "That's between you two." "I don't take sides." But *there is no neutral ground in abuse*. Their refusal to acknowledge reality forces survivors to carry not just the weight of the abuse, but the added burden of being the sole witness to their own experience. When reality has only one witness, the inevitable gaslighting becomes *trivial*.

The Active Enabler: Extended Arms of Abuse

Where passive enablers perfect invisibility, active enablers embrace visibility as agents of the narcissist's will. Functioning as extensions of the abuser's reach, they make escape impossible by eliminating safe spaces and destroying any potential refuge.

Family friends, my brother, my stepfather, and others mastered this role. Any news shared by me, good or bad, always ended with detailed intelligence reports delivered back to my mother—even before going no-contact. Every struggle I shared became ammo. Every small victory, a target.

They weren't just enabling abuse—they were actively gathering the materials for its construction. A text from my brother wishing my wife and infant daughter would "hit a fucken *[sic]* tree and die," wasn't anger. It was programming, perfectly executed.

These enablers often compete for favored status by demonstrating their usefulness to the narcissist. Delivering messages that can't be delivered directly. They punish boundary-setting with deliberate precision. They transform family gatherings into interrogations, or casual conversations into intelligence-gathering. Their participation isn't reluctant—it's *enthusiastic*, driven by the rewards of being part of the narcissist's inner circle.

Covert Enablers: False Allies in Sheep's Clothing

The covert enabler represents a sophisticated threat because they appear as allies while functioning as saboteurs. They perfect the art of concern-trolling, wrapping their enabling in the language of care and support.

"I understand why you're hurt," the family friend would say, voice dripping with sympathy as I described my mother's latest campaign. She'd listen with apparent compassion, validate my pain, create the illusion of support. Then, inevitably: "But she's your *mother*. She won't be around forever. Don't you think you'll regret this?"

This type of enabler causes damage because they access our vulnerability under false pretenses. We open ourselves to them believing we've found understanding, only to discover we've handed fertilizer to another agent of the system. They use our trust to plant seeds of doubt, to nurture guilt, to water the shame the narcissist planted. Their betrayal cuts deeply because it comes disguised as care.

Institutional Enablers: Sanctioned Complicity

Causing what may be the most widespread and far-reaching damage are the institutional enablers—therapists, religious leaders, legal systems, and social structures that provide official sanction for abuse. They transform personal pathology into systemic oppression by lending their authority to the narcissist's narrative.

How many therapists, purportedly trained in trauma, spend countless sessions trying to convince us that forgiveness is *necessary* for healing. Not understanding, processing, or safety, but forgiveness? Delivered to abusers like gift certificates for future harm. These professional enablers are particularly dangerous because they come with credentials that make their unknowing obstruction look like well-meaning wisdom.

"Honor thy father and mother," religious counselors intone when seeking guidance about protecting children from the poison of our parents. No context. No nuance. No acknowledgment that honoring might mean preventing generational trauma transmission. The institution's need to preserve its image—the happy family, the intact congregation, the redemption narrative—supersede any obligation to protect the vulnerable.

These enablers don't just fail to help; they actively harm by providing abusers with righteous justification. They transform boundary-setting into sin, self-protection into selfishness, escape into abandonment. Their participation elevates personal abuse to cosmic significance. Now, you aren't *just* defying your abusive parent, but your God, society, the natural order itself.

The family court system that suggests "family therapy" with the abuser or that forces victims to coparent with someone who thrives on chaos and control? Institutional enabling. The extended family that insists "blood is thicker than water," while ignoring that blood can carry pathogens? Cultural enabling. The social structures that prioritize family preservation over individual safety? Systemic enabling—on a civilizational scale.

Malignant Enablers: Architects of Secondary Abuse

The malignant enabler represents perhaps the most diabolical category—those who comprehend the abuse system's architecture not as unwitting participants or fearful collaborators, but as opportunistic engineers who recognize its utility for their own psychological campaigns. These aren't confused allies or anxious appeasers. They're conscious architects who see the existing narcissistic infrastructure and think, "Perfect, I can use this."

Sam Vaknin—a controversial but influential voice in narcissistic abuse survivor communities—describes what he calls narcissistic collusion in his extensive writings. While his work is debated in clinical circles, his concepts have proven valuable for many survivors trying to name their experiences. Vaknin suggests situations where individuals with narcissistic structures recognize each other's patterns and form temporary alliances when their goals align. This parallels more established clinical perspectives from Otto Kernberg's work on malignant narcissism and Jürg Willi's writings on collusive relationships. The pattern, whether we call it collusion or confluence, remains consistent: two predators who normally compete suddenly coordinate when they spot particularly valuable prey.

Where other enablers might claim ignorance or good intentions, the malignant enabler operates with *full knowledge and deliberate intent*. They understand precisely what they're doing when they breach decades of no-contact, when they hand over carefully guarded information, when they facilitate access to victims who've spent years building walls. Their participation isn't accidental—it's *weaponization*.

The shared fantasy Vaknin describes becomes particularly relevant here—when a malignant enabler encounters an existing narcissistic abuse structure, they don't challenge it. Instead, they recognize its utility and join the alternate reality, adding their own distortions to the echo chamber. The supposed friend who witnesses years of your systematic protection strategies, your carefully maintained boundaries, your hard-won distance from an abusive parent or partner, and then makes the deliberate choice to collapse those defenses? They're not misunderstanding the situation. They're *exploiting* it.

The ancient proverb *the enemy of my enemy is my friend* holds as true as it ever has.

These enablers recognize the specific wounds left by narcissistic abuse in their victims—and deliberately trigger them. They understand that *reintroducing past trauma creates present destabilization*, making you easier to control, gaslight, or position as the "difficult" one who cannot maintain relationships. They see the scar tissue and know *exactly* how to reopen those wounds.

The malignant enabler often exhibits what Paulhus and Williams describe in their work on the **Dark Tetrad**—narcissism, Machiavellianism, subclinical psychopathy, and sadism converging in a personality structure that views relationships as chess games and people as pieces. But unlike the primary narcissist, they don't need to be the sole source of abuse. They're content to harmonize with existing dysfunction, creating what Vaknin calls an *echo chamber of abuse* where multiple reality-distorting voices make truth impossible to discern.

"I was just trying to help," they'll claim, after orchestrating a reunion they knew would be devastating. "I thought enough time had passed," they'll say, having deliberately waited for your most vulnerable moment to strike. Their language divulges the game—always positioning themselves as hero or peacemaker, holding their hands behind their back, with a book of matches in one... and a Molotov cocktail in the other.

What distinguishes malignant from covert enablers is the *absence of genuine care* anywhere in the equation. They're not merely flying monkeys unknowingly doing the narcissist's bidding, but what Vaknin calls **flying proxies.** They are *conscious collaborators* who don't just understand the game, but play it for their own purposes. They don't just enable the original narcissist—they create a *secondary layer of abuse* that compounds the original trauma while maintaining plausible deniability.

Once you recognize the pattern, it cannot be unseen. Consider a common, yet devastating scenario: The intimate partner who understands a survivor's entire trauma history, who has witnessed the careful architecture of protection they've built over years—sometimes decades. Now imagine them deliberately and methodically dismantling those protections and inviting the poison back in. Not through unknowing carelessness but by cold, cruel *design*. This creates what Vaknin describes as a **dual mothership** where two narcissistic structures converge on a single victim, each reinforcing the other's distortions, making reality itself negotiable.

The neurological impacts compound *exponentially*. When someone who knows your entire trauma history consciously chooses to weaponize it, your hippocampus doesn't just struggle to consolidate—it fragments entirely. The anterior cingulate cortex—our brain's conflict monitor—already overtaxed from processing the original abuse, now faces a second-order betrayal that defies categorization.

While other enablers are driven by recognizable—if dysfunctional—human needs like fear or belonging, the malignant enabler operates from a different psychological blueprint entirely. In the next section, 'The Psychology of Collusion,' we will dissect the unique motivations that drive these conscious architects of secondary abuse.

Taking a Moment: Map the Patterns in Your Life

Take a moment to map your own system. Which of these enabler types are present? Write down their names or roles (e.g., 'Aunt S.,' 'Family Friend B.') and one specific memory that illustrates this behavior.

Seeing the patterns can help you break free of them.

II.

The Psychology of Collusion

Searching for Answers

Whether it's autistic pattern recognition, hypervigilance as a trauma response—or both—I have a *need* to dig into the reasons behind these things. To find the *why* even the enablers may not fully realize. It's been nearly two years since having this journey of self-discovery foisted upon me by repetition compulsion and the resurfaced emotional memories of a traumatic childhood. In that time, I've made understanding the neuropsychology behind these systems a *special interest.* From this point, things take something of a turn towards scientific synthesis. Stick with me, though, I think you'll find it enlightening.

Understanding the psychology doesn't diminish the impact, however. Whether malice or self-preservation, intention is irrelevant.

Regardless of reason, being thrown under the bus... hurts.

Fear-Based Enablers: Your Sacrifice, Their Safety

Fear-based enablers operate on a simple formula: it's easier to sacrifice you than confront the narcissist. They've learned through painful experience that resistance brings retribution, so they participate in your scapegoating to barter for their own safety.

My stepfather exemplified this dynamic. After years of being my mother's primary target, he discovered that her rage toward me meant respite from his own torment. His participation in her campaigns wasn't malicious. For him, it was survival.

These enablers often use phrases that reveal their intention: "Don't rock the boat." "You know how she gets." "Just apologize. Keep the peace." "Be the bigger person." "He's making everyone miserable." Each statement acknowledges the abuse while simultaneously *demanding you absorb it for everyone else's comfort.* They know the narcissist is wrong. They just find it easier to convince you to accept the wrongness than to challenge it themselves.

Watch how quickly they turn when you refuse to be the sacrifice anymore. The family members who seemed sympathetic when you were absorbing the abuse become vicious when you step out of the firing line. Suddenly, you're not the *victim*—you're the *problem*. You're "tearing the family apart" by *refusing to be torn apart yourself*.

Favor-Seeking Enablers: Competing for Crumbs

Some enablers participate not from fear but *appetite*. They've tasted the intoxicating feeling of being in the narcissist's good graces and become addicted to that special status. These enablers compete for favor by demonstrating their usefulness, and nothing proves loyalty like participating in the destruction of the designated enemy.

Some friends or family members may brag about being in the narcissist's "inner circle," about being trusted with special information (likely salacious gossip about *you*), about being chosen for privileged treatment. The price of admission? Enthusiastic participation in whatever campaign is being run against the victim. These enablers will trade your peace for their position, your safety for their status, your children's wellbeing for their continued access as narcissistic supply.

This type reveals how narcissistic systems create artificial scarcity— love, approval, and safety become limited resources that must be competed for rather than freely given. The enablers learn to see other family members—not as fellow victims—but as competitors for resources. Your pain becomes their opportunity. Your exclusion ensures their inclusion.

The cousin who suddenly develops opinions about your parenting after being welcomed into the narcissist's confidence? Favor-seeking. The sibling who escalates attacks on you whenever their own status feels threatened? Favor-seeking. The extended family who performs cruelties as tests for loyalty? More of the same.

Like poorly trained puppies, they are all competing for breadcrumbs from the narcissist's table.

Trauma-Bonded Enablers: The Captive Collaborators

Perhaps most heartbreaking are the trauma-bonded enablers, those who participate in abuse while genuinely believing they're protecting the abuser. Their own victimization has created such profound cognitive distortion that they see the narcissist as fragile, wounded, in need of protection from the cruel world that refuses to understand them.

My stepfather, my maternal grandparents, and a few others put on a superb show of this. Beyond their fear-based enabling lay *genuine conviction* that my mother was misunderstood, that her cruelty stemmed from her own pain, or that I was at fault because my boundaries represented additional wounds to her already damaged psyche. In my grandparents' case, this was done without ever acknowledging that they were the ones who caused that damage. They couldn't see that their protection enabled her destruction, that their compassion for her eliminated any possibility of safety for the rest of us.

These enablers often share their own versions of the narcissist's abuse stories as explanation for their behavior. "She had such a terrible childhood." "He never learned how to show love properly." "They're doing the best they can." This framework transforms abuse into understandable response, cruelty into complicated love, systematic destruction into a generational tragedy. One that must be *endured* rather than *ended*.

The trauma bond creates a peculiar blindness where, like the narcissist, the enabler literally *cannot see* what healthy people see. Show them a recording of abuse, and they'll explain how it's love. Present them with evidence of harm and have it reframed as misunderstanding. Their own survival depended on this reframing for so long that they've lost the power to see reality without an accountability-masking distortion filter.

Architect Enablers: Build on Your Wounds

Where the fear-based enabler is motivated by survival and the trauma-bonded enabler by distorted loyalty, architect enablers, such as the malignant subtype above, operate from a psychology of pure, planned *opportunism*. Their actions are not a reaction to the narcissist's power; *they are a co-opting of it.* They see the wounds inflicted by the primary abuser not as a tragedy to be soothed, but as a pre-excavated foundation upon which they can build their own structures of control.

For them, the psychological payoff is a profound sense of superiority. They become unseen puppeteers in dramas of their own creation— manipulating both the primary narcissist *and* the targeted victim while maintaining the clean-handed facade of a concerned bystander. This is not enabling. It is the covert construction of a secondary labyrinth that *intersects* with the first, creating a *psychological kill box* where every escape route from one predator leads directly to another.

Their psychology can be understood through the clinical lens of the Dark Tetrad of personality traits described earlier. Their Machiavellianism is the engine of their strategy, allowing them to view people as pawns and relationships as transactional games to be won.

Their own narcissistic traits fuel their need for this covert, coercive control, allowing them to derive immense supply from being the secret, powerful force directing the drama, while subclinical psychopathy provides the necessary lack of empathy. This is the chilling void that allows them to see your carefully constructed boundaries not as a sign of health, but as a *challenge to be dismantled.* They do this not only without any remorse for the devastation they wreak, but while making you believe *you're the problem.*

This mindset explains the predatory nature of their timing. They have mapped your vulnerabilities like tidal charts. Not with empathy, but with the dispassionate eye of a military strategist. The psychological drive is to strike when the target is most depleted and resistance is lowest, thereby maximizing their own impact. They don't merely follow the primary narcissist's script, but piggyback onto it and creatively write new scenes into the drama—scenes that always, without fail, *amplify chaos*. That this is usually done under the guise of facilitating healing adds to their need for plausible deniability. Deniability is required, for these individuals are deathly allergic to accountability.

Ultimately, their goal is to induce a state of *fragmented vigilance* in their victim. By creating a multi-front war, they ensure the amygdala never rests, oscillating between different threat signatures until the victim's nervous system can no longer establish a stable defensive position. These are not the same puppies competing for breadcrumbs, but *scavengers* and artists of mimicry. Ones who have learned to hunt in the wake of another's destruction— understanding that wounded prey is the easiest to take down. They don't seek the narcissist's approval, but they require the narcissist's damage to create the optimal conditions for their own sadistic games.

For my autistic brain, understanding the *why* behind this collaboration is crucial. But to understand the unique damage they inflict, we must turn to the neuroscience of betrayal itself.

III.

The Trauma of Betrayal

The First Cut's Not Always the Deepest

One manner of trauma only recently being mapped by neuroscience emerges not from the primary wound, but from the discovery that those we trusted to witness, validate, or protect us were instead *complicit in our destruction*. This is what Dr. Jennifer Freyd first identified as *betrayal trauma* in her groundbreaking 1996 work. Betrayal trauma represents a unique neurological event, *distinct from the narcissistic abuse itself*. When the person we depend on for survival is also our source of danger, the mind performs an extraordinary bifurcation—simultaneously knowing and not knowing, seeing and not seeing.

My journey's revelations extend beyond Freyd's framework into something more complex: what happens when betrayal becomes *environmental*, when it's not singular but *systemic*, when nearly every potential ally reveals themselves as a *double agent?* This isn't just betrayal trauma—it's *betrayal infrastructure*. One where the very architecture of family becomes a booby-trapped maze of false doors and trap floors.

The Neurological Signature of Systematic Betrayal

Our brains process betrayal trauma differently than primary abuse. When the narcissist attacks, our threat detection systems activate predictably—fight, flight, freeze, fawn, as Pete Walker outlines in his seminal work on complex PTSD. But when an enabler betrays, something more complex occurs.

The hippocampus, attempting to consolidate memory, encounters a paradox: this person is simultaneously safe and dangerous, ally and enemy, witness and denier. The resulting fragmentation isn't just psychological—it's neurological, creating what Bessel van der Kolk describes in The Body Keeps the Score as a particular form of complex trauma where memory itself becomes unreliable. The enablement furthers the narcissist's efforts to shred our reality-testing.

Let's look at the less, but still all-too-common scenario of an intimate partner in this context. Over years of no-contact with a narcissistic parent, the partner still occasionally delivers airstrike coordinates to the narcissist, ultimately introducing them to the victim's children, violating every boundary put in place to protect them from the person behind their psychologically devastating upbringing. A malignant enabler does this while simultaneously adopting—and pushing—the narrative that there was no childhood abuse, that the victim is "crazy."

That is not simply retraumatization.

It's the discovery that escape was always an illusion, that the very person who represented potential freedom was, in fact, another bar in the cage. The amygdala, encountering this betrayal, may undergo what we might understand metaphorically as a recalibration—resetting baseline threat detection in ways consistent with Stephen Porges's polyvagal theory, where safety itself becomes suspect as a category.

Research by Bush, Luu, and Posner on cognitive and emotional influences suggests the anterior cingulate cortex can become hyperactive when processing conflicting information. In betrayal trauma, this region may struggle particularly hard to reconcile irreconcilable realities.

Where betrayal trauma from other enablers creates that paradox of "safe yet dangerous," the malignant enabler creates something more sinister: the *complete dismantling* of safety as a concept.

Partner as protector, partner as betrayer. Partner as shelter, family as storm. The result of our brain's inability to grok this isn't mere cognitive dissonance, but a *catastrophic cognitive collapse*, in which the very categories we use to navigate reality reveal themselves as false constructs.

The Temporal Collapse of Betrayal Discovery

When we discover enabling—particularly historical enabling—*time itself collapses*. Every memory requires reexamination through this new lens.

That aunt who never saw anything wasn't absent; she was selectively blind. That therapist who pushed reconciliation wasn't misguided; they were potential recruits. The childhood memories of family dinners transform retroactively—what felt like chaos reveals itself as orchestration, what seemed like individual cruelty exposes itself as collective choreography.

This temporal collapse creates what Judith Herman describes in *Trauma and Recovery* as a unique form of grief. Not just for what was lost, but for what *never existed*. We mourn imaginary families, fictional support systems, and the phantom allies we constructed to survive. The discovery of this systematic enabling doesn't just wound the present; *it retroactively wounds the past*, transforming every moment of safety perceived into betrayal, postponed.

The Metabolic Cost of Betrayal Recognition

The body keeps score, as van der Kolk's pioneering work reminds us, but betrayal trauma creates a particular somatic signature. The dorsal vagal shutdown that occurs when we recognize enabler complicity isn't temporary—it can become *architectural*, as Porges explores in his work on neurophysiological foundations. Our nervous systems, designed for binary threat assessment, struggle to process the double-agent nature of enabler betrayal. They are family, yet enemy. They are present, yet absent. They are seeing, yet blind.

This creates what we might understand as a biological "exhaustion of ambiguity"—systemic fatigue that may stem from the metabolic cost of constantly assessing and reassessing trust. Every interaction requires triple processing: what is said, what is meant, what will be reported. The cognitive load of maintaining this constant translation can deplete resources needed for healing, growth, and connection, consistent with Robert Sapolsky's comprehensive documentation of chronic stress responses. We become our own hypervigilant surveillance system as we monitor for signs of enabler activation, or the subtle linguistic shifts that signal recruitment.

Emerging research by Andrea Danese and James Baldwin on inflammation following interpersonal trauma suggests the immune system may mount distinct responses to betrayal—though these findings remain preliminary and require further investigation. What we can say with more certainty is that the stress of navigating enabler networks creates measurable physiological impacts that compound the original trauma.

The Epistemological Violence of Gaslit Reality

When enablers deny witnessed harm, they commit yet another atrocity against the narcissist's victim: *epistemological abuse*. This psychological violence is an assault on the victim's capacity to know reality, extending beyond the enabler's gaslighting or the narcissist's confabulation into something more fundamental: the organized destruction of a victim's *epistemic authority*—the right to be a reliable narrator of one's own experience, as Miranda Fricker explores in her work on epistemic injustice.

The child who suffers abuse in full view of relatives who "see no evil, hear no evil" learns not just that they won't be protected, but that their own perception cannot be trusted. If everyone denies what you clearly experienced, the fault lines run not through family but through consciousness itself. If reality is negotiable, memory becomes suspect, and the self fragments into observer and observed, each doubting the other.

This creates a particular vulnerability to future manipulation. Having learned that consensus reality trumps personal experience, survivors of enabler betrayal often struggle to trust their own judgment, as Herman documents extensively. They seek external validation for internal experience, require witnesses to confirm their wounds, need documentation to believe their own memories. The enablers didn't just fail to protect; they damaged the very apparatus of self-protection—the ability to trust one's own perception.

The Immunological Metaphor

Betrayal trauma creates what I recognize as an "autoimmune disorder of trust". Just as autoimmune conditions cause the body to attack its own tissues, betrayal trauma causes the psyche to attack its own capacity for connection, as Freyd and Birrell explore in their work on betrayal. The system designed to create bonds becomes the system that prevents them.

The resulting hypervigilance that develops *isn't* paranoia—it's *pattern recognition* born from the necessity to survive. When those who should protect become those who expose, when confidants become informants, when sanctuary becomes trap—the only rational response is systematic suspicion.

But this protective mechanism becomes its own prison, where the walls we build to keep out enablers also keep out genuine connection. The surveillance system that detects potential betrayal also prevents authentic intimacy.

In the case of malignant enablers, what we find ourselves dealing with goes further still, to trust's *complete systemic failure*. The psychological immune system doesn't just attack healthy tissue; it shuts down entirely, recognizing that the very mechanisms of connection have been weaponized beyond repair. What Vaknin calls "narcissistic contagion" spreads through the entire system—victims become perpetrators, enablers become abusers, and the original dysfunction *metastasizes* until escape seems impossible.

Healing the Betrayal Wound

Recovery from betrayal trauma requires what it simultaneously makes impossible: to trust in the face of evidence that trust... kills. This paradox *cannot be resolved* through logic but must be metabolized through experience (not the experience of perfect safety, for that is fantasy) but the experience of proportional risk, planned vulnerability, and proxy relationships that honor both connection *and* boundaries, as Brené Brown explores in her research on vulnerability and courage.

Neuroplasticity research offers hope—the brain's betrayal detection systems, while hyperactive, remain malleable, as Richard Davidson and Bruce McEwen demonstrate in their work on social influences on neural change. Through careful titration of trust, through relationships that consistently honor boundaries, through experiences of being believed, validated, and truly seen, the nervous system can be reeducated to learn not every connection is a trap, not every confidence is ammunition, not every ally is a potential enemy.

But this healing requires what my journey and the journeys of others has made clear: the courage to release those who choose complicity, to grieve the family that never was, to build chosen families based not on biological obligation, but proven reliability.

The path forward isn't through forgiveness of betrayal. It lies in the recognition that some wounds teach us who to trust with our healing, and who to release to their own uncomfortable darkness

Dancing Lessons

Betrayal's wounds may take on many forms—
What you think of first may be bad, for sure.
Some, in plain sight ignore all social norms—
The worst? Disguised from view—and scar much more.

Coming from those whom we expect to trust—
Be it a partner, parent, priest, or pal.
For an act this vile, love isn't a must—
The worst offenders invent rationale.

They will dance a dance, while singing a song—
This isn't, I swear, something comical.
These actors and their ilk can do no wrong—
You see... It's psychopathological.

One must be prepared for the turns and twists—
When navigating life with narcissists.

IV.

The Playbook

The Normalization Campaign

Enablers excel at normalizing the abnormal and making the unacceptable appear inevitable. They deploy phrases designed to erode your sense of reality: "That's just how she is." "He means well." "You're too sensitive." "Every family has problems."

This systematic normalization minimizes the abuse, making you question whether you are overreacting. It universalizes the experience, suggesting everyone deals with this level of dysfunction. Most importantly, it forecloses the possibility of change—if this is "just how she is," then resistance is futile.

The impact compounds over time. Survivors, their reality testing tattered, begin questioning their own reactions, doubting their own perceptions, and wondering if they are, in fact, the problem. The enabler's steady drip of normalization erodes the bedrock of self-trust that makes resistance possible. You start accepting the unacceptable because everyone around you treats it as not just acceptable—but *expected*.

I spent decades thinking verbal violence was just how families joke around. That comparing your child to a mass murderer was just dramatics. That wishing death on infants was something born out of love. The normalization was so complete that it took *years* of self-work and therapy to recognize that this *wasn't normal*. It was systematized cruelty, cosplaying as family tradition.

Blame Shifting and Victim Targeting

When normalization fails, enablers pivot to blame-shifting. The abuse itself becomes less important than your reaction to it. The focus shifts from what was done to you to what you did to "provoke" it. This is where DARVO makes an appearance.

Coined by Jennifer Freyd, DARVO stands for "Deny, Attack, Reverse Victim and Offender." This method of rhetorical trickery is one that toxically abusive people use to steer you away from the real issue and make you feel like you're the problem. And it's one of the hallmarks of a narcissistic abuser. Enablers are quick adopters of this tactic, as well.

"What did you do to set her off?" "You know how to push his buttons." Questions like these contain the embedded assumption that you are responsible for managing the narcissist's emotions and behaviors. Your failure to successfully navigate their minefield becomes the real problem, and not that the narcissist surrounded you with landmines in the first place.

This creates double victimization—first the abuse itself, then the blame for causing it. Enablers find it easier to control the victim than confront the abuser, because whether they feign blindness or lacked awareness, they do indeed bear witness—and nobody wants to become a victim of the narcissist's rage themselves by standing up for the downtrodden.

Instead, they focus their energy on pressuring you to become more manageable. They can't make the narcissist reasonable, so they try to make you more accommodating.

They can't create safety, so they demand you accept danger.

Information Warfare

Functioning as intelligence networks, enablers gather and transmit information making true escape impossible. They master the art of casual interrogation, extracting details through conversation with the appearance of innocence, but which later become weapons in the narcissist's arsenal.

"How's work going?" becomes reconnaissance about your financial stability. "Are you seeing anyone?" becomes intelligence about potential support systems. "That's a nice neighborhood" becomes information passed on about your location. Every detail shared in good faith becomes ammunition for those who act in bad, and are squirreled away by the narcissist for future psychological warfare campaigns.

For the narcissist, information is ammunition—*and they'll take it any way they can get it.*

Recovery Sabotage

It can seem narcissistic abusers possess radar for vulnerable moments in recovery. Just when you're making progress, just when boundaries start holding, just when therapy begins working—they feel their control slipping. How convenient that this is when their enablers appear with perfectly timed interventions designed to derail healing.

"Don't you think you're being dramatic?" they ask when you start therapy. "You seem angry," they observe when you begin setting boundaries. Claiming "This isn't like you," or "you've changed," when you stop accepting the unacceptable. They question your choices or lay guilt on you for your healing practices, minimize your progress, amplify your setbacks, and present reconciliation as the only path to peace.

Timing is what reveals the systematic nature of their intervention. The narcissist monitors for signs of escape and mobilizes their network to prevent it. Your healing is a threat to the system these enablers are invested in maintaining, so they work to pull you back into familiar dysfunction. They prefer you complacent. Compliantly broken—over healthy and boundaried.

The Enabler Recognition Checklist

As an autist, I like lists. They help me see patterns, even when my nervous system is flooded. So, here's your guide to spotting enablers—before they spot your vulnerabilities.

Red Flags (Active Enabling):
- Asks detailed questions about your life but shares nothing meaningful about theirs
- Conversations feel like depositions disguised as coffee catchups
- Always steers discussions back to the narcissist ("How's your mother?" "Her heart is breaking," etc.)
- Minimizes abuse you've shared ("I'm sure she didn't mean it that way," "you know how she is.")
- Gets defensive over boundaries you set with the narcissist
- Sudden contact after periods of silence (especially during conflicts)
- Uses fear, obligation, and guilt (FOG) as a primary communication tool
- Shares your confidential information without permission
- Their "concern" always leads to the same suggestion: *reconciliation* ("Just talk to them.")

Yellow Flags (Passive Enabling):
- Claims neutrality in obvious abuse situations (Reminder: There is no neutrality when someone is being abused!)
- Selective memory about witnessed events
- "I don't want to get involved" is their mantra (And yet... they are.)
- Present during abuse but "didn't notice anything"
- Deflects direct questions about the narcissist's behavior
- Uncomfortable when you discuss your healing journey
- Suggests you're "dwelling on the past," that you should "just let it go."
- Never validates your experience without adding "but..." (Thus invalidating it!)

Manipulation Tactics to Watch For:

- **The Guilt Sandwich**: "I care about you," "I just want everyone to be happy"
- **The Time Bomb**: "They won't be around forever," and "You'll be sorry when they're gone!)"
- **The False Equivalence**: "You've both made mistakes"
- **The Selective Historian**: Only remembers the "good times"
- **The Burden Shift**: "This is really hard on everyone"
- **The Flying Monkey Special**: "I'm just the messenger"
- **The Human Garbage Pie** (My favorite!): A bitter dish, topped with all of the above.

Sample Scripts for Boundary Setting

Something noteworthy about boundary conversations with enablers—they're trained to see your justifications, arguments, defensiveness, and explanations as an invitation to debate. So don't JADE (Justify, Argue, Defend, or Explain). Be a broken record. Be the gray rock they can't squeeze blood from. Be *boring*.

Initial Boundary Setting:

- "I won't discuss my relationship with [narcissist/abuser] with you."
- "That topic is closed for discussion."
- "I've made my decision and it's not up for debate."
- "This isn't something I'm willing to talk about."

When They Push (And They Will):

- "I've already answered that."
- "My boundary hasn't changed."
- "Asked and answered."
- "No is a complete sentence."

The Nuclear Options (When Nice Stops Working):

- "This conversation is over. I'm hanging up/leaving now."
- "I won't be responding to communications about [narcissist/abuser]."
- "Contact me again about this and I'll block your number."
- "Your disrespect of my boundaries has consequences."
- "If that's all you have to discuss, we don't have anything to talk about."

For the Guilt-Trippers:

- "Your feelings about my boundaries are yours to manage."
- "I'm not responsible for your comfort with my choices."
- "My decision stands regardless of how it makes you feel."

For the "But Family!" Crowd:

- "Family doesn't get a free pass to harm me."
- "DNA isn't a license for abuse."
- "I define what family means to me."

Warning Signs Someone is Becoming an Enabler

People do not usually start as enablers. They are recruited—slowly boiled like frogs who don't notice the water temperature rising. Watch for these progression patterns:

Early Stage - The Recruitment Phase:

- Suddenly included in narcissist's confidence
- Begins receiving "special" information about you
- Their language about you starts shifting
- Develops opinions about situations they weren't part of
- Starts parroting narcissist's phrases or concerns

Middle Stage - The Activation Phase:

- Tests your boundaries with "innocent" questions
- Becomes defensive of narcissist's behavior
- Minimizes or reframes abuse incidents
- Increases contact during your conflicts with the narcissist
- "Devil's advocate" becomes their favorite role

Late Stage - Full Enabler Mode:

- Actively takes part in campaigns against you
- Spreads false information or twisted narratives
- Emotional investment in forcing reconciliation
- Sees your boundaries as personal attacks
- Cannot acknowledge any wrongdoing by narcissist

The tragic thing? Sometimes you can watch it happening right in front of you. The cousin who used to understand becomes another flying monkey. The friend who validated your experience starts suggesting you're "too harsh." The sibling who escaped with you gets sucked back in and suddenly you're the enemy for staying *free*.

Green Flags: Identifying Genuine Support

After a lifetime in dysfunction, genuine support can feel foreign. Here's what actual allies look like:

They Respect Boundaries by:
- Never pushing for reconciliation
- Not needing explanations for your decisions
- Honoring requests not to share information
- Accepting "no" without debate or guilt trips

They Validate Without Minimizing:
- "That sounds really difficult"
- "Your feelings make complete sense"
- "I believe you"
- Never follow validation with "but..."

They Support Your Healing Journey by:
- Celebrating your progress
- Not sabotaging your therapy work
- Encouraging your growth—even when it changes dynamics
- Seeing your boundaries as healthy, not problematic

They Maintain Consistent Support by:
- Not vanishing during conflicts
- Not reporting back to the narcissist
- Keeping your confidences absolutely
- Offering steady support, regardless of family pressure

They Model Healthy Behavior by:
- Having their own boundaries
- Not triangulating or creating drama
- Taking responsibility for their own emotions
- Demonstrating genuine empathy without agenda

The Ultimate Green Flag:

Real support isn't transactional. It doesn't come with strings, conditions, or expiration dates. Real support doesn't require you to sacrifice yourself for family harmony, nor does it demand you set yourself on fire to keep others warm. The ultimate green flag may be the easiest to see, and for those of us raised in these systems, one which can be difficult to accept: We feel not guilty, but *safe*.

Taking a Moment: Practice Makes ... Doable

Review the 'Sample Scripts for Boundary Setting.' Which one feels the most difficult for you to imagine saying? Which feels the most empowering? Practice saying one—or all—of them out loud to yourself.

What feelings come up?

V.

The Mirror Check

Recognizing Yourself in the System

Perhaps you've reached this section with creeping recognition—not of others' behavior, but your own. The uncomfortable possibility that you might be functioning as an unwitting conduit in someone else's abuse system. This recognition itself represents the beginning of systemic awakening, the moment automatic processes become visible for examination.

The Gossip Gateway

Information trafficking often begins innocuously—sharing "concern" about someone's choices, discussing family "drama," passing along updates that seem harmless but carry hidden payloads. The narcissist doesn't announce their intelligence-gathering operation; they initiate through worried questions, concerned observations, casual curiosity about people you both know.

Watch for these patterns in your own behavior:
- Sharing information about someone who's explicitly gone no-contact with the person asking
- Passing along details about someone's life without their permission
- Finding yourself saying "Don't tell them I told you this, but..."
- Noticing the person consistently asks about specific individuals during your conversations
- Feeling a subtle thrill from being the one "in the know"
- Rationalizing disclosure as "keeping family connected" or "they have a right to know." Spoiler alert: *You aren't, and they don't.*

The systemic tell: When someone consistently transforms your conversations into intelligence briefings about others, you're being recruited into a reconnaissance infrastructure.

The Triangulation Test

Enablers often become vertices in triangulation patterns without recognizing their geometric function. You become the third point that stabilizes dysfunction—the messenger, the mediator, the bridge between parties who've established boundaries for good reason.

Ask yourself:

- Am I delivering messages between people who won't speak directly?
- Do I find myself explaining one person's position to another?
- Am I being asked to "help them understand" someone's boundaries?
- Have I become the go-between for conflict I didn't create?
- Am I maintaining relationships that only exist through me as conduit?

When you become essential to communication between two adults, or forced to use another as a go-between yourself, you've been roped into pathological trigonometry.

Scripts for Declining Participation

When you recognize potential recruitment:

For the Information Gatherer:
- "I don't feel comfortable sharing information about [person]."
- "They can tell you themselves if they want you to know."
- "That's not my information to share."
- "Let's talk about something else."

For the Message Carrier:
- "I can't be the messenger between you two."
- "You'll need to communicate with them directly."
- "I'm not comfortable being in the middle of this."
- "This conversation needs to happen between the people involved."

For the Concern Troll:
- "If you're worried, you should talk to them."
- "I trust them to make their own decisions."
- "Their choices aren't my business to discuss."

The Rehabilitation Protocol

If you recognize yourself as an unwitting enabler, the path forward requires both cessation and repair:

1. **Immediate cessation**: Stop information flow immediately. No gradual weaning, no "one last update." Put a cork in it. Now.
2. **Boundary communication**: Inform the narcissist that you won't be discussing the other person anymore. Expect pushback, guilt-trips, claims of betrayal, potentially even a smear campaign. Look at this as confirmation. Your discomfort is evidence of correct action.
3. **Potential warning**: Consider whether to inform the person whose information you've been sharing. This requires careful evaluation—will it help them protect themselves or merely add to their burden? **Be Warned:** Regardless of how sorry you may be, you are not owed forgiveness, and may lose or permanently damage the relationship.
4. **System examination**: Investigate how you became susceptible to recruitment. What needs did this role meet? Belonging? Importance? Conflict avoidance?

The Deeper Recognition

The most profound realization for unwitting enablers may be that your participation wasn't moral failing so much as it was system functioning. Narcissistic abuse systems recruit through manipulation of normal social processes—desire for connection, conflict avoidance, information sharing, or family loyalty. These aren't character flaws, but human tendencies *weaponized against collective wellbeing*.

The gossip that seems like bonding, the message-carrying that feels like helping, the information-sharing that appears as concern—these represent the system's genius for disguising harm as care, surveillance as connection, and intelligence gathering as intimacy.

Taking a Moment: Check Yourself

Have you been an unintentional enabler? Have you been caught in a triangle of drama? Have you been a spreader of gossip? I only mention the unknowing varieties of enabler for this inquiry, because the malignant subtype won't seriously entertain these questions in relation to themselves.

However, for most people, the willingness to engage in this self-discovery means whatever the result: all is not lost.

It may bother us to find we have been used. We may feel violated at the discovery we've been an unwitting pawn in someone else's game of chess. It is not only OK, but *important* to make these discoveries about ourselves—we don't know what we don't know, after all! The more important part is what you do with this newfound knowledge.

VI.

Strategic Response

Protecting Yourself from the Network

Standard boundary advice fails with enablers because they're invested in boundary erosion. You can't reason someone into respecting limits they are committed to violating. Instead, protection requires strategy in its approach.

While anyone can fall victim to emotional, psychological or narcissistic abuse, it's my admittedly anecdotal experience that when it comes to enablers, those exhibiting even a modicum of developed emotional intelligence tend to recognize and respect the boundaries of others, while also keeping a healthy supply of their own, making them less likely to be a "flying monkey," or other enabling type. Additionally, people exhibiting strong narcissistic traits tend not to form (or maintain) friendships with "healed," or emotionally mature individuals because their boundaries make them difficult to control.

Put potential enablers on an information diet. Immediately. Share nothing that could be reported back that you don't want weaponized, especially if it's something important to you, or something you're vulnerable about. Enablers have proven they'll trade your confidences for narcissistic approval, so give them nothing to trade. Your job? Your relationships? Your healing? None of their business. Your response to everything becomes "Fine." "Good." "Nothing new."

Master the gray rock method. Become boring, unresponsive, utterly without intelligence value. "Everything's fine." "Nothing new." "Same old, same old." Repeat until they stop fishing. You want to be so boring they'd rather watch CSPAN than interrogate you.

For as helpful as the Gray Rock methodology can be in many situations, if you really need to interact with such people on a slightly deeper level (co-parenting and caregiving for aging or ill family members are but two examples), the "Yellow Rock" method may have greater success than its monochrome cousin. Think of Yellow Rock as Gray Rock with a bit of color injected in the form of mild politeness—still not revealing anything worthwhile for the narcissist, just less stand-offish.

Though gray and yellow rocking can be successful, and for as much as these phrases are thrown around in survivor forums and media, these methods will not work for everyone. You will be well advised to take some time and evaluate what your abuser's reaction might be to your suddenly less forthcoming self. As information about you becomes harder to come by, expect the narcissist to step up their game—and expect the enablers to do the same.

It may also be prudent to practice your responses and give yourself some grace as you explore trying them out. When it comes time to try it out, don't be surprised should you find yourself shaking like a leaf, your heart about to leap from your chest.

Please don't just attempt either method if you fear for your physical safety from either your abuser or their enablers. Reach out to your local domestic violence shelter or call the national domestic violence hotline at 1-800-799-7233 in the US, or 0808-2000-247 in the UK. There are people trained to understand what you're experiencing, to believe you, and who may be able to offer options you won't think of on your own. I speak from personal experience in this, and as difficult as that call is to make, it *can* help.

Create distance *without announcement*. Don't declare you're pulling back—just do it. Gradually increase response times. Slowly decrease visit frequency. Let the relationship fade to whatever level keeps you safe. They'll notice, but explaining gives them something to argue against. Remember—don't JADE, and "No," is a complete sentence.

Document everything. Enablers gaslight too. Keep records of conversations, save texts, screenshot social media posts. Not for them—for you. For those moments when they try to rewrite history and make you question your own memory. They're unlikely to care about your receipts, but you'll be glad you have them.

Build networks outside the toxic system. The narcissistic family system is so interconnected that anyone inside remains suspect until proven otherwise. True support often comes from chosen family—people who understand abuse dynamics through experience or education, who respect boundaries as basic human decency, not special accommodations.

Operational Security: Mapping the Network

> The watermarking technique described below requires careful consideration. Do **NOT** use this tactic if:
>
> - You face risk of physical violence or escalation
> - You're in active litigation where discovery could misconstrue your intent
> - Your therapist or domestic violence advocate advises against it
> - You're already experiencing overwhelming cognitive load This is a short-term detection tool only—not a sustainable strategy.

Whether family or mutual friends, leaving the entire network behind is often the safest move to make. There are those for whom this may not be immediately possible, if ever. For those with no option to escape the narcissistic system, knowing who—if anyone—to trust, becomes paramount.

When you suspect but can't confirm enabler activity, strategic information management becomes essential. Think of this as watermarking your reality the way Hollywood watermarks screenplays—introducing controlled variables to test the integrity of your communication channels.

The technique operates through deliberate, traceable disclosures. You share specific details—real or fabricated—with individual suspects, then monitor for echoes returning through the narcissist's behavior or communication. Not for purposes of deception, but for *detection*. A way to map invisible networks through the wake of information.

Consider this example: You mention to a suspected enabler that you're considering a job change to a specific company—one you have no actual intention of pursuing. Weeks later, the narcissist suddenly develops opinions about that exact company, perhaps mentioning a friend who had terrible experiences there. The watermark has revealed the channel.

Or perhaps you share different false timeline details with different suspects—telling one person you're planning something in March, another in May. When the narcissist's interference arrives timed to one specific date, you've identified your leak.

The complexity requires documentation. Without notes tracking what you've told whom, you risk losing your own thread in the labyrinth of strategic disclosure. *The cognitive load this requires cannot be understated*, nor can it be sustained. The mental resources consumed by maintaining multiple tracks simultaneously are just one hidden cost of extreme narrative OpSec.

I cannot recommend this as a long-term strategy—but if it's something you feel up to, it deserves a place in your arsenal. If you go this route, *proceed with caution.*

VII.

The Path Forward

Embracing Necessary Losses

The hard truth about escaping narcissistic systems is that leaving the narcissist often means losing the entire network. Enablers are invested in the system's continuation; your healing threatens their equilibrium. They'll choose the devil they know over the uncertain freedom you represent—nearly every time.

This loss extends beyond simple relationships. You lose the mythology of family, the comfort of belonging, the identity derived from your place in the system. You grieve not just the relationships you had, but the relationships you *thought* you had, the support you *believed* existed, the safety you imagined was possible if you just wanted it enough.

It *is* hard. It *does* hurt. It *will* be worth it.

Here's what my journey has taught me: *what we lose was never real.* The support that evaporates when you set boundaries was always conditional. The love that required self-sacrifice was always transactional. The belonging that demanded your destruction was always toxic.

No-contact remains, for many survivors, the most protective path to healing—though each person's circumstances are unique. Cultural obligations, co-parenting requirements, eldercare responsibilities, or financial constraints may make complete separation impossible. In such cases, modified approaches like structured contact, gray rock techniques, or carefully boundaried interactions may be necessary. The goal isn't perfection but protection— finding whatever level of distance keeps you and your loved ones as safe as possible within your specific constraints.

The Reckoning

Narcissistic abusers and their network will frame your boundary-setting as the violence. Your self-protection as selfishness and your escape as abandonment. That's what enablers are defending—narcissistic logic at its purest—where victims are portrayed as villains who use boundaries as bullets.

In place of quantity, build *quality*. A few genuine relationships do more than eclipse dozens of enabling ones—they help you grow into who you're meant to be. Find people who validate your experience without requiring proof, who respect your boundaries without argument, who support your healing unconditionally, and who see your refusal to accept abuse as the strength it is, not the stubbornness or control of the narcissist's narrative. There are fewer of these people out there than there should be, but more than I ever expected to find.

Success isn't measured by family reconciliation or enabler awakening. It's measured by your own peace. By your children's safety. By the gradual quieting of internalized voices demanding you sacrifice yourself for others' comfort, and by the increasing spans of time where you forget to feel guilty for choosing survival.

You broke the cycle. You chose the hard path of personal truth over complicit comfort, of safety over approval, and of your children's future over your family's past. You refused to be another enabler in the generational chain of connivance. That refusal—that magnificent, necessary refusal—is the greatest gift you can give: to yourself, to your children, to every future generation that will grow up free from the poison you refused to pass along.

Let the enablers keep their careful blindness, their calculated betrayals, their comfortable collusion. You've chosen the harder path of clear sight and clean conscience. While they remain frozen in their enabling patterns—like Dante's traitors in ice, unable to weep or change—you generate warmth through truth-telling, boundary-setting, and the stubborn insistence that love without safety isn't love at all.

Their playbook was written in fear and sealed with silence. Yours is written in courage and shared with those ready to see. That's the difference between enabling and healing—one perpetuates darkness while the other generates light. And light, once introduced, puts patters that were always present into sharp relief.

The Hot Seat only burns if you agree to sit in it. The game only continues if players show up. The system only survives if enablers enable. Your refusal to participate isn't just personal freedom—it's systemic disruption. Every boundary you hold makes their world less stable. Every truth you tell makes their lies less tenable. Every healthy relationship you build proves their dysfunction isn't inevitable.

They'll call you the problem. Difficult. Unforgiving. The destroyer of family unity. Wear those titles like the badges of honor they are—because authenticity will always be a threat to a system that functions through facades. In a sick system, the healthy person always looks crazy. In an empire of lies, the truth-teller is always the traitor.

Let them keep their Hot Seats and their cold hearts. You've got better places to be, healthier people to love, and a future that doesn't require you to bleed for belonging. That's not mere survival, it's what freedom looks like. And your victory, unlike their Pyrrhic ones, creates space for others ready to win freedom of their own.

This book ends here, but your story continues—make it one worth telling.

Then, shout it from the rooftops.

After

Asking 'How could you?' but not asking 'Why?'
Friends, family, neighbors: You always knew.
Did she threaten to rain fire from the sky,
For you to just accept her slanted view?

New life blooms as you waste; you'll harm no more.
Death's silence now comes for your forked tongue.
Yours hurt you, mine hurt me. Not anymore.
When the casket closes, spring will have sprung.

In the wake of storms, the sun always shines,
After battle—in the quiet, birds sing.
Glaciers recede, a valley's green defines.
From the ashes, after flames, new trees spring.

Free of you now, there are families three.
The hurt, the pain, the rage — it ends with me.

Glossary

Betrayal Trauma: The specific neurological and psychological wound that occurs when someone we depend on for survival or safety becomes our source of danger. Identified by Jennifer Freyd (1996), it represents the mind's paradoxical attempt to simultaneously know and not know, creating fragmentation that goes beyond simple trauma into something that fundamentally breaks our reality-testing apparatus.

Cognitive Collapse: Not mere dissonance but the complete collapse of the categories we use to navigate reality. When partner-as-protector and partner-as-betrayer occupy the same space, the mind doesn't just struggle—it fragments.

DARVO: Deny, Attack, Reverse Victim and Offender. Jennifer Freyd's acronym for the rhetorical sleight-of-hand narcissists use to make you the problem. A three-step dance where your abuse becomes your fault and your abuser becomes your victim.

Enabler: Anyone who, through action or strategic inaction, maintains the architecture that allows abuse to continue. They're the engineers aiding the narcissist with their alternate reality construction project.

Epistemic Violence: The assault on your capacity to know reality. When enablers deny witnessed abuse, they don't just gaslight—they attack your fundamental right to be a reliable narrator of your own experience. Based on Miranda Fricker's concept of epistemic injustice (2007).

Flying Monkey: Borrowed from *The Wizard of Oz*, these are the narcissist's minions who do their bidding, often without realizing they're being used. They deliver messages, gather intelligence, and execute attacks while believing they're helping.

FOG: Fear, Obligation, and Guilt—the trinity of emotional manipulation. Coined by Susan Forward, it describes the atmospheric pressure narcissists and enablers create to keep you compliant.

Gaslighting: Systematic psychological manipulation designed to make you question your own perception, memory, and sanity. Named after the 1944 film *Gaslight,* where a husband deliberately drives his wife to question her reality.

Gray Rock Method: Becoming so boring, unresponsive, and emotionally flat that you offer no narcissistic supply. You become the conversational equivalent of watching paint dry—deliberately.

Hot Seat: My maternal family's post-dinner torture ritual disguised as entertainment. One person becomes the target of "jokes" designed to demolish while everyone watches, participates, and calls it love. Refusal to participate makes you the next target.

JADE: Justify, Argue, Defend, Explain—the four things you should never do with narcissists or enablers. Coined by Al-Anon, it recognizes that these responses are invitations to debate rather than boundaries to respect.

Malignant Enabler: My term for those who consciously recognize and exploit existing abuse architecture for their own purposes. They're not confused or scared—they're architects of secondary abuse who see your wounds as opportunities.

Narcissistic Collusion: Sam Vaknin's term for when multiple narcissistically-structured individuals recognize each other's patterns and form temporary alliances, creating echo chambers of abuse where reality becomes completely negotiable.

Narcissistic Supply: The attention, admiration, emotional reaction—positive or negative—that narcissists require to maintain their false self. You're not a person, but a human battery.

No-contact: The complete cessation of all communication and interaction with an abuser or their network. Not low contact, not gray rock—total removal from their reach. Often the only way to heal.

Repetition Compulsion: The unconscious drive to recreate familiar trauma patterns, even when they're destroying us. We don't just remember our wounds—we reenact them. We unconsciously seek out relationships and situations that mirror our original injuries. The child who learned love through chaos becomes the adult who mistakes intensity for intimacy.

Shared Fantasy: Vaknin's concept of the alternate reality narcissists create where their grandiose self-image is real and you exist only as a prop in their psychological theater.

Trauma Bond: The biochemical attachment that forms between abuser and victim through intermittent reinforcement—unpredictable cycles of abuse and affection that create addiction-like dependency.

Triangulation: Using a third party to manipulate, control, or destabilize a relationship. The narcissist's geometry where you're never allowed direct communication, always filtered through someone else.

Yellow Rock Method: Gray rock's slightly warmer cousin—maintaining boundaries and information diet while adding just enough polite pleasantness to avoid escalation. Can be useful when complete disengagement isn't possible.

Bibliography

Brown, B. (2012). *Daring Greatly: How the Courage to Be Vulnerable Transforms the Way We Live, Love, Parent, and Lead.* Gotham Books.

Bush, G., Luu, P., & Posner, M. I. (2000). Cognitive and emotional influences in anterior cingulate cortex. *Trends in Cognitive Sciences, 4* (6), 215–222.

Danese, A., & Baldwin, J. R. (2017). Hidden wounds? Inflammatory links between childhood trauma and psychopathology. *Annual Review of Psychology, 68*, 517–544.

Ronningstam, E. (2005). *Identifying and understanding the narcissistic personality.* Oxford University Press.

Vaknin, S. (2015). *Malignant self-love: Narcissism revisited* (10th rev. ed.). Narcissus Publications. (Original work published 1999)

Paulhus, D. L., & Williams, K. M. (2002). The Dark Triad of personality: Narcissism, Machiavellianism, and psychopathy. *Journal of Research in Personality*, 36(6), 556–563.

Međedović, Janko; Petrović, Boban (2015). The Dark Tetrad: Structural Properties and Location in the Personality Space. *Journal of Individual Differences*. 36 (4): 228–236.

Kernberg, O. F. (1991). Aggression and love in the relationship of the couple. *Journal of the American Psychoanalytic Association*, 39(1), 45–70.

Kernberg, O. F. (1995). *Love relations: Normality and pathology.* New Haven, CT: Yale University Press.

Willi, J. (1984). *Couples in Collusion: The Unconscious Dimension in Partner Relationships.* United Kingdom: Hunter House.

Christie, R., & Geis, F. L. (1970). *Studies in Machiavellianism.* Academic Press.

Davidson, R. J., & McEwen, B. S. (2012). Social influences on neuroplasticity: Stress and interventions to promote well-being. *Nature Neuroscience, 15*(5), 689–695.

Freyd, J. J. (1996). *Betrayal trauma: The logic of forgetting childhood abuse.* Harvard University Press.

Freyd, J. J., & Birrell, P. (2013). *Blind to betrayal: Why we fool ourselves we aren't being fooled.* Wiley.

Fricker, M. (2007). *Epistemic injustice: Power and the ethics of knowing.* Oxford University Press.

Herman, J. L. (1992). *Trauma and recovery: The aftermath of violence—from domestic abuse to political terror.* Basic Books.

Danese, A., & Lewis, S. J. (2017). Psychoneuroimmunology of early–life stress: The hidden wounds of childhood trauma. *Neuropsychopharmacology, 42*(1), 99–114.

Johnson, S. M. (2019). *Attachment theory in practice: Emotionally focused therapy (EFT) with individuals, couples, and families.* Guilford Press.

Linehan, M. M. (2014). *DBT Skills Training Manual* (2nd ed.). Guilford Press.

Spring, C. (2019). *Recovery is my best revenge: My experience of trauma, abuse and dissociative identity disorder.* Carolyn Spring Publishing.

Porges, S. W. (2011). *The polyvagal theory: Neurophysiological foundations of emotions, attachment, communication, and self-regulation.* Norton.

Sapolsky, R. M. (2004). *Why zebras don't get ulcers: The acclaimed guide to stress, stress-related diseases, and coping.* Holt.

van der Kolk, B. A. (2014). *The body keeps the score: Brain, mind, and body in the healing of trauma.* Viking.

Walker, P. (2013). *Complex PTSD: From surviving to thriving.* Azure Coyote.

Appendix

For Clinicians & Helpers: A Quick Reference

Assessment Questions to Identify Narcissistic Abuse:

- "Who in your life consistently respects your boundaries?"
- "When you set a limit, what typically happens?"
- "Are there people who seem to know things about you that you didn't share with them?"
- "Do family members pressure you to reconcile with someone who has hurt you?"

Red Flags in Your Own Practice:

- Feeling compelled to advocate for family reconciliation
- Minimizing a client's abuse experiences as "miscommunication"
- Suggesting forgiveness before safety is established
- Using phrases like "but they're your mother/father"
- Assuming all family relationships can be healed

Therapeutic Stance for Narcissistic Abuse Survivors:

- Validate first, explore later
- Safety before processing
- Boundaries before reconciliation
- Stabilization before family work
- Client autonomy over family unity

Avoid These Interventions:

- Confrontation sessions with suspected narcissistic abusers
- Family therapy where power dynamics are severely imbalanced
- Forgiveness work before trauma processing
- Pushing for "understanding the abuser's perspective" prematurely

Acknowledgements

A.L., A.C., J.V. & Z.J. for music.
A.N. for unceasing encouragement.
S.H. for lighting the path to Happiness.
E.R. for showing me what safety feels like.
K.J. for patience, support, and smiles.
W.C. for belief, honesty, counsel,
and residential permanence.
RD for Sangha

www.ingramcontent.com/pod-product-compliance
Lightning Source LLC
Chambersburg PA
CBHW052102270326
41931CB00012B/2858